ON MY WAY

First published in 2006 by
The Dedalus Press
13 Moyclare Road
Baldoyle
Dublin 13
Ireland

www.dedaluspress.com

© Desmond O'Grady, 2006

All rights reserved. No part of this publication may be reproduced in any form or by any means without the prior permission of the publisher.

ISBN 1 904556 42 6 (paper)

Dedalus Press titles are represented and distributed in the USA and Canada by Dufour Editions Ltd., PO Box 7, Chester Springs, Pennsylvania 19425, and in the UK by Central Books, 99 Wallis Road, London E9 5LN.

Front cover photograph by John Minihan
Design by Pat Boran

Printed and bound in the UK by Lightning Source, 6 Precedent Drive, Rooksley, Milton Keynes MK13 8PR, UK

The Dedalus Press receives financial assistance from An Chomhairle Ealaíon / The Arts Council, Ireland.

ON MY WAY

Desmond O'Grady

ACKNOWLEDGEMENTS

Acknowledgement is made to Poetry Salzburg at the University of Salzburg for publishing some of these poems in *The Wide World, A Desmond O'Grady Casebook* edited by Wolfgang Görtschacher and Andreas Schachermayr, Salzburg, 2003. *Summer Harvest Renga* was published by Maximus Press, Kinsale, Cork, Ireland, 2004. Thanks are also due to the editors of the literary reviews and magazines where others of these poems appeared, including 'Ageing Siren I' which appeared in *The Road Taken*, University of Salzburg Press, 1996.

The author is grateful to John F. Deane and Pat Boran for publishing *On My Way* in times of changeover at the Dedalus Press and is grateful also to the poet Matthew Geden for co-reading and co-correcting the proofs.

The author and the Dedalus Press wish to express their thanks to Gisèle for her permission to reproduce her drawing of Desmond O'Grady, and to John Minihan for his permission to reproduce his photograph of the author on the cover of this book.

*Dedicated
to my children
Deirde   Leonard   Gisèle*

Contents

Yes Or No	1
Vocation	2
Siren	3
Love Dance	4
Today	6
Marriage	7
Son	8
Lines in a Roman Schoolbook	9
A Sculptor in Rome	11
Hospital	12
Friends	13
The Well	14
My Room	15
One Week	17
Summer Harvest Renga	21
Profiles	25
Mill Stream Bridge	26
Hallowe'en	27
Makers and Breakers	28
Passerby	29
Last Call	30
Arrival	31
Old Age	32
Mr Shanabu in Alexandria	33
Alexandria Elegy	35
Goodbye Alexandria	37
The Poet C.P. Cavafy's Mother	38
Spring Holidays	39
Joseph Brodsky Visits	40
The Painter Gisèle	41
Italy	44
Her Birthday Night	47
May Day	49

Horse	50
Crosstalk	51
Autumn Festival	53
Michael Hartnett 1941-1999	54
Dream	56
Olga Jwaideh O'Grady 1930-2000	57
Self-Portrait	58
Seasons	64
The Battle of Kinsale 1601	65
Voices	69
My School English Teacher	71
Friendship	74
Old Haunts	75
Sea Change	76
Whale	77
This Island	79
Grandson	80
Winter in Sevilla	81
Friends at Funerals	83
Ageing Siren Concerto	84
Hermit and Harlot	87
Time Passes	88
Old Satyr	89
Crow and Poet	90
Love	91
My Muse	92
Lady Raffaella	93
The View	95
New York 2001—Baghdad 2004	96
The Old Head Of Kinsale Says	98

Drawing of Desmond O'Grady
by Gisèle, 2000

Yes Or No

Sometimes one's life faces a yes or no
answer if one is to survive progress.
The quick to yes one need never regress,
gets due reward, then lives as most must do.

The one says no's left dead, quick forgotten:
must bide dear time, face each day's start anew
to live and grow one of that refined few
who shape a mode of life because self-chosen.

Vocation

Vocation varies; where we tend to prodigal,
how we take and give our own example:
the Occident, the Orient, or both;
whether or not to cut our personal cloth.

Initiation grants us place among
like aspirants. We each chant our song
while we keep faith; may mature to hymn.
Some stay in choir. The rest change voice, go dumb.

As postulants we've time to meditate
upon our choice of life and to collate
what was left, what taken. Both texts evaluated
we may decide to stay, or change our mind.

With ordination we apply what's learned
from the contents and consecrate what's miracled.
Some may scripture what inspires vocation,
to sacrament its value and its duration.

Siren

She surfaced here by chance. She'll dance all night
among we boys and girls as if on wing
with love. By day, her stroll the village street
brings song to old men's minds, smiles to the young.

Statuesque her carriage. Obsidian black hair
falls down her shoulders like unrolled manuscripts.
Gracious her face. Balanced her features there.
Those eyes reflect love's oriental markets.

Her icon nose ascends from mounted cheekbones
flanked by seashell ears, kissed, whisper back.
Her lips the sides of a half-open book of poems
will tell the pages' contents should she speak.

That a tabernacle of her mouth contains
the sacred mystery of love's secret smile.
The column of her neck stands pure Dorian
on sculpted scapula mount her cupola breast-hill.

Her stroll's a glimpse of some Grecian statue
that moves and gives when her sanctuaries close.
A man would live his three lives out in virtue
of the hope that her sanctuary's all his.

All I behold smiles in her eyes were mine
a while and sirened me through my life's sail.
Now they sing out to my lone heart again
and swing my sail's gib for that shore, her soul.

Love Dance

Upset,
you cleared off
without words.

All morning I moped
restless absence, lunched
alone from cans.

Nervous afternoon.
Unable to able,
I played patience.

Evening.
Went back west
to a place. Diversion.
They danced. I drank.

Seaward a wrinkled
tree trunk, a fist
of white cottages,
a frieze of fishingboats.

Suddenly you, there,
in the crowd, radiant.
You took a room here
to live the night alone.

We nodded recognition,
no more. They danced.
You danced. I watched.

Then; ripe, ready,
I gave you the nod.
We danced. All night.
Without words...

Moon set. Sunrise.
Calm as dawn we
strolled to your room
facing the sea,
without words.

Today

Today I am the seabird
       blackbacked, wheeling
       half high in the sky
       up any cliff's side.

Today I'm the seabird
       grey-breasted, solitary
       at that evening hour after sunset
       when we'd speak with strangers.

Today I'm the heron fisher
       plunging salt estuaries
       long before birdtraps
       or slingshots.

Today I'm the gull that refuses
       to stand on one leg
       and flies like lost envelopes
       blown from the pockets of messengers.

Today I'm the flat-headed sea crow
       that wings round the heart's headland
       and drops in its glide as the fiddlebow
       drops down the melody playing it.

Today I'm the common small sparrow
       in the fo'c'sle of a foreign trader
       tied up in a white harbour
       perched by a head of green basil
       in a rusty tincan for good luck.

Marriage

On their own day,
in the fullness of their seasons,
they married –
were hallowed in one,
purified in all that the word
gives life to, without
wrinkle, without disfigurement.

No longer two—one flesh
in high mystery. Woman's
body and man's flesh
make singular substance.

What has been so joined
cannot stand sundered.
This primal fellowship
fears no forfeiture
in punishment of any fall,
under any flood's destruction.

May the wife grow
fruitful as the vine,
the children sturdy as olive.
May they witness
their children's generation
and may their ageing
hold all they desire
in peace.

Son

My son holidays
from school for Easter,

tall in youthful shyness.
He takes his Sunday saunter

round to the open sea
straight into the risen sun.

At the foot of a green headland
he stands, faces the ocean.

Adolescence angles his day
as the waves' tumble talks him in.

He drops his clothes on the ground,
walks into the sea and the sky.

With a simple sense of ritual
he swims through the swell with youth.

Wading ashore nakedly natural
he stands straight as truth.

Some girl watches from the headland,
what she thinks not yet understood.

Lines in a Roman Schoolbook

I

From this, our garden of the growing mind,
from this school campus where our green dreams,
hopes and futures grow, and seed, and grow,
we look down this valley where the green
world seeds and grows perennially. The view
looks much the same as twenty five years
ago—I was a boy and elsewhere—when another
mortal, local or exile, looked him down;
or twenty five centuries ago when some
anonymous traveller, to or from the town –
Etruscan, Roman, Gaul—paused and looked and
passed through this valley's theatre to his future.

II

This introspective exile here today
is minded of his elsewhere: its occasions
twenty five decades ago when poets were hedge
school masters in my fields and kept alive
the way of life that's ours by conversation –
just as that other hedge school master talked
in his muddled marketplace under the Attic sun
and paid the price extorted. The best seems always
based on solid dialogue as when, when young,
our elders passed on to us what they knew,
then passed us on to those who knew the more –
for space shapes no restriction round its star.

III

The inherited daily terror of the nineteenth century's
blind educational vision that was ours, and
ours—corporal punishment, the bully's power,
regimentation—you and yours are spared.
There's health in young revolt and alienation
consolidates the strength for self survival
when you graduate to the school of hard knocks
on the slopes of the vale of tears; makes more sense too
of those universities of companionship we converse in.
And we have found in the productivity of routine
the geometry that shapes our days' fulfilment –
a method and a meaning clear and clinched as Euclid.

IV

In the valleys of the future we shall walk
and talk through, growing on good conversation
and the memories of good conversation; in the last
library of memory, reflection, thought we settle in
overlooking the valley of darkness and light; in the seed
time of our time, on our way home to the last town,
we may pause, like that ancient anonymous traveller,
at the entrance to the theatre of the last valley
prepared to conduct our last discourse, to say:
We talked and told each other all we knew,
as ours with theirs and theirs, since that Greek start;
taught those after us to do the same for their part.

A Sculptor in Rome
to Herzl Emanuel

Your theme is man's destruction of man redeemed
by his rebirth through faith in life with love.
Whether your figures lie dead or in their love life,
or stand at pause in human silence screamed,
they raise the next in line above their state
or reach in hope for life beyond our now.
Friends' busts and heads surround these in a row:
children, grownups, the aged. Survivors of fate.

Your peoples' history inspires your work
while portraits of your choice reflect your view
of others who lived their own lives around you.
Its nature reads ineluctably atavistic
of you or us. What speaks is form made live
by discerning eyes that background relief.

Hospital

That alien hospital awaits. I'm afraid. Not
of the operation but of the loneliness of wards
I've known visiting hospitalized friends ailing,
dying. In hospital there's a sterility in that machine
of method and manners frustrates the giddy
imagination. And those gaunt faces staring,
bed after bed, ward after ward, as in concentration
camps staring. It's a compound of loneliness
visitors feel loath to stay long in—hardly
arrived anxious to leave. Except, perhaps, women.
They sit, as in church, in their resigned patience,
or lie, like taking a late morning in bed at home,
or as though in old-fashioned staying at home.

My only other hospital time I was seven after
that accident the night before my First Communion.
Was there an omen in that fall? So many falls since.
No hospital for those but time, endurance. No
plastic surgery of the spirit for those scars.

Friends

After yesterday's long sailing,
landfall, hours' talk over dinner,
last night's deep sleep,
we walk my island.

This stony road by the sea's edge
we've covered before—for a few
fish baked in the open on a clay
pot at the road's end.

Where two roads join we plunge
into the flesh-refreshing wave.
Free laughter. You're married now.
Dry. Dress. Talk of our bread-winning
world—brackish waterhole in memory.

Later with friends over fish soup—
the floating fishhead minds me of
past working winters—we swap
yarns. There's a bond in friendship
quarrels no question, asks no answer.

The Well

A small thick-walled house
of white stone on a hill
surrounded by stony fields
under the bright moon.

A flag-stone terrace all round
and nearby a good well, a date
and your grandfather's name
carved on the marble lip.

Down below, the shine of the sea
under the stars. We talk
of our grandfathers, of fathers,
the life of the land, the lost old ways.

Also carved on the well's rim this verse:
Anyone passing by here
who drinks the water from this patriot's well
forgive old father Chaniotis.

I who have passed, stopped
and have drunk here gratefully,
remember and forgive your grandfather
in the name of my own two.

My Room

I

Four white walls
two windows, half-door.
Ceiling of bamboo,
seaweed, mud.

In one corner
an old iron bed;
in another, drawers
with books on top.

My table,
on which I live,
stands against the window
fronting the sea.

Through the window facing me
low white houses
clustered like gulls.
Beyond, the hills distend
in tawny folds into the sky's haze.

Through the window at my elbow
the bay, sea, and the sun
setting behind Mount Vigla.

I've climbed that mountain,
swum that sea.
In this room I love
my woman, fathered my son,
create my country
people my panorama.

II

On the wall of my room
hangs a small picture
of a sailboat sailing dark
seas into a shadowed sun
that's neither rising nor setting.

It reminds me of childhood
when I'd go down to gaze
at the rare ship that sometimes
sailed into the abandoned port
up north I come from, where
I daily dreamt of far off cities
white and huddled like crystals
in bright sunlight by blue seas
fringed by waving palms.
I planned to sail there one day.

Here, in this harbour, among
this huddle of foreign fishermen's
white cottages, on this blue sea,
at times, I remember, long for,
that abandoned port up north.

One Week

Monday

Ground rocky,
sky gull empty.
No land wind.
Sea wind blew
all week.

Last night
changed bed
from sunset
to sunrise,
day's sides.

Three longboats
frieze at anchor,
rock, ready
for wind drop.

Tuesday

Barren fields
without water.
One well,
brackish.

The sun's blaze
blinds light.
I make
my mind's
rest place,
line stones

one by one
as children
play house.

Noon's blaze
blunt hands,
broken nails
grope rocks,
make wall
lines, shape
my start.

Wednesday

Desolate headland.
Death damp house.
No match strikes.
No lamp lights.

Outside
curved moonlight
cradles boat bows
as my palm
your bare breasts.

Thursday

A thousand miles from you
time's long wave lopes this bay.

I write your name in the sand.
Time's wave washes it away.

My memory of your body
burns as the sun in the sky.

My cravings for you burn
in this, my body's urn.

Friday

Your eyes
move in moonlight
as leaves move
in night's breeze
through windbreak.

Two boats
ride anchor,
that third
sails far
from us.

Landlocked
on land's end,
our spread tree
umbrellas.

Saturday

In a deserted tavern
by the sea's edge,
under the night sky
moon and pilot star,
colour of sea shell
under still water,
an ageing couple dance

till dawn alone to
love's mouth music.
Lovers in old age cut
figurines in moonlight.
May we, when the storm
of survival has abated,
dance likewise.

Sunday

He said: Once visited
a man lives haunted thereafter.
Again he said, at his end: the price
he paid he reckoned too high. . .

To learn stability
from those stable;
good fellowship
from good fellows.

No friend: "Have all you wish
but let us have peace amongst us."
He friend, three years in Dachau,
living it up as though back
from the dead like Lazarus.

I have been some time dead
this Easter Week, must
resurrect now or never.

Summer Harvest Renga
written with Matthew Geden

July is every farmer's
month to reap and bind
what he sowed in spring

    the sun in her hair
    she walks the shore

that dove's chant this morning
welcomes a sky blue day
to enjoy a natural life

    wisps of seaweed twist and turn
    to the music of the sea

this dolphin surfaces and dives
in his neighbour's bay
to undulate her wavelets

    ripples in the river ride
    all summer is movement

sailor a nymph ashore
each hot summer
to heat chill winter

    warmth as temperatures rise
    in the surge of salt water

if on the other hand she's earthy
make hay while the sun shines
to feed all natural appetites

    flowers fill the hedgerows
    with colourful lust for life

select the lovers the season offers
to decorate your life
and heat your winter's home

    sudden squalls and storms
    pass by mere strangers

retreat from all bad weather
to personal security works well
for productive activity

    light splash of rain on face
    sprinkle of conversation

then ashore from the ocean
find time to boat and walk
god's rivers lakes and streams

    making it up as you go
    brief exchange of words

pause at times
to look at enjoy
the reality of nature

    observe now an old man
    making hay between showers

nature in summer bloom
surrounds my walk by the river
watch the fish dance underwater

    following your footsteps
    tap out the seasonal beat

rise the croaked chorus of crows
from the church graves
the palaver of pigeons from ruins

    sibilant sweep of the seashore
    shingle shudders in sunshine

wild birds in bushes choir in song
and solo voice rises to lyric pitch
in the air and in my soul

    patterns emerge from repetition
    visitors come and go

at the end of the river and stream
lie down in the green
and sip from the spring

    bars fill with music and talk
    the songs of summer

remember the enlightenment
write it down to encourage
others who will take example

    lightness of touch in each new day
    maintain routine and ritual

pleasure of fresh fantasy
adventures of the imagination
create life daily

    incoming tide washes away
    yesterday's footprints yesterday's fears

here the river flows out
into the ocean under
the setting sun

    at twilight slowness is all
    time to think

evening darkens to night
as stars of past
and present blink

    eyelashes flicker
    as light fades

memories blink from their distances
until cloud and night
covers with darkness

    somewhere a door shuts
    the harvest is done

Profiles
after Ugo Foscolo, *To Evening*, 1778?-1827?

Because perhaps we still engage each other
I still court thoughts of you here in these
our mortal evenings. Should you
reject your vague horizons that fade in space
and come to live here, our seasons'
instruments would orchestrate our quiet
disquiets, harmonize our silent praise. Daily
invoked, arrive and meander the last
secrets of our hearts' ways for the joy of it.
Your absence wanders my dreams' old routes
to the nowhere of our imaginations' horizons.
Let us annul our deaths, allow our restless
hearts forget for good what's irrelevant in our lives.
To honour our serenity that warrior spirit
which combats within me will rest in peace.

Mill, Stream, Bridge

Morning in the countryside. Autumn works its relentless
process. Summer's green ages, fades out. About me all
decays. Weak sunlight strengthens little, even ourselves.

Leaving you to the occupation of your own space, I set out
to walk the land, follow those cart ruts that bind the lee side
of that fallow field, pass that masked-green frog pond
clothed with weeds; once the dream love meeting place
of a prince and princess, now a bad dream to face daily.
Bubbles burst in that muddy water, gasp questions, as do
epiphanies of imagination's galaxy. I nightmare our son
might topple in there, drown. May God forbid that curse.

Enter the autumnal wood. Pigeons scatter through the branches
like my thoughts. I follow the trail that leads through brambles,
underbrush, low boughs intertwined like arms in affection's hold.
Occasional donkey dung marks direction. Autumn light
permeates what's deciduous about me, as your physical
or psychic presence does. Far off the gunshots of hunters.

Over the hill. Shuffle down towards the gully and stream.
Break open ground at their humpbacked, stoneknuckled bridge,
overgrown with weeds. Sight of the abandoned mill ahead
shadowed by a tree. You and I considered living in there
with ourselves. Arrived I squint through dirty windows
at the fortress we might have made a castle by loving in it.
Rickety table, broken chair, fallen bed, bottles in fireplace.
A lovepair of squirrels scuttles along a crossbeam.
Life still in these shadows we might have lovelit.
I close my eyes, leave. What silhouettes our life stalks me.

Redetermined I recross bridge and stream, reclimb the hill
through the skeletal trees, return to our hosts' home and to you.

Halloween
for Patrick and Ursula Creagh

Halloween weekend and this year's harvest
of life and death. We escape our city world
for the country and your autumnal farmhouse.
Honest joy of friends' visit to friends for old
times' sake. Glasses of welcome. Sit to the feast.
Eat and drink well with toasts to past and future,
then settle round the open fire in three generations.

Now disguised, our scarum children play games,
dare each other poke frightened fingers at shadows
on walls at Find the Fairy. The grandmother evokes
old times, ghosts and games of her own childhood.
We muse round the cauldron hangs on the flames,
share hopes and fears of the magic that outside
brews for the growing generation around us.

The fire burns down. The dog outside howls
at the moon for entrance. Lanterns reflect thoughts
of dead friends in our last glass of hot punch.
It's time to throw salt in corners, ashes and water
out on the dead land, place cross on door, light candle.

Corncobs decorate our bedposts. "Good night.
Don't let old ghosts fright. Hold your fernseed tight".

Makers and Breakers

> Carrara. White marble heart
> of Italian sculpture. Quarried
> daily since Roman times.
> 'The statue is in the mountain'.

To a chant they deliver their boulders from their mountain's belly,
square, then clean the marble as workable blocks and slabs.
Guided by the model's drawn lines, sculptor and masons hammer
their chisels' chip to carve shapes clear, then sand to smooth.
The finished work stands a poem or prose statement in stone,
articulates the marble's indigenous language through form.

Given my way of seeing, you're scattered about this stoneyard
as those fragments that once promised our wholeness, harmony
and radiance but now lie lifeless round me, their spirit deserted.

With similar purpose, but using pen and paper, I try to delineate
your now gone elsewhere presence here with my scribal
relief of words in lines on this white page. In imagination's quarry
I had envisioned your light rose travertine shaded lips,
deepwater golden, sunbrown onyx of your flesh; dark velvet
in your southern eyes; translucent marble that's your smile.

> Found once, then lost.
> Your scattered image lies
> about my word yard.
> The poem is in the imagination.
>
> 'Our emotions are not skilled workers'.

Passerby

Back from my life elsewhere, I gaze down
across this plain stretched towards my ocean.
Beside that distant town out near the coast
stands your family's summer house. We last
stayed there before my going away to take
the dare made to myself. That began our break.
Now back I view our lost lives' shuffle since then.

You must still spend summers in that home
more, now your daughter and two sons have grown.
Have they made you a grandmother since, times over?
I have fathered my girl and son elsewhere,
who too will grow and live their choice of dreams.
Will they meet yours? We never knew our times
would cross, connect, then never meet again.

Last Call

The bush telegraph works. Your news
with its urgency came by boatman to my
here remoteness via people you'll never meet
in this foreign to you country. I dropped
everything at once and made it, in time,
twenty four hours later, thanks to friends.

This hour comes to all, once. *Father dying
come home.* You didn't think I'd make it. Home
now, I find him low but stubborn. Life. Death.
The meandering mind of old age. And yet,
that old humourisity still. To go out on a joke.
Should we let him to out in his own joke time
or force his flight? Go in peace, not in pain?
Aware, not comatose? Has man a right, some
responsibility, to help man go? This, my solitary's
return road to origins and originator, saddens.
Slán agus go n-éirigh an bóthar leat.
May the road rise with you.

Arrival

I find you there on that alien hospital bed
asleep with your false teeth half slipped out
of your sagged mouth. Your skin a fine
linen stretched tight over your skull
reminding me of the skulls found in old
abandoned graveyards as an adventure-hunting
boy. This is the beginning of your end I've not
wanted to think about face on but now must
face. What may we say to our dying fathers, expect
our sons to say to us dying? Later, outside in sun,
we sons discuss the practicalities of your going:
coffin, grave, tombstone, distribution of possessions.
Also if, when my day comes, they're to bring me
home or put me down where I fall abroad.

Old Age

You've pulled through again, at least
physically for now and, though your meandering
mind wanders more and worse, you're out
of that concentration ward and in a happy
home. We only feared your wandering
out on the road, like one of the children,
and getting bashed into eternity as Florence's
father did walking home to his Italian village
from American Boston. At least you're home,
yet might get the notion to go back again
to your birthplace too on foot, or cheat
and try to drive your car. Disaster that!
The pity of the stubborn mind dying cell
by solitary cell; the stubborn rowing
with married children; irritation
with growing grandchildren who cannot
understand. King Lear's old gaga story. He
wandered off too but had a faithful
caring Fool to talk to, watch for accidents.
Not you, too reserved always to make close
friends or suffer fools gladly. The solitary aged
seem seldom beautiful to behold—those vacant
eyes, peeling hands, sagged jaw or tight mouth.
Only in the fresh transparency of death
does a youthful freshness return, ironically.
Is recovery more desirable than painful release?

Mr Shanabu in Alexandria

I

Mid fifties. Five foot eight erect. Broad shoulders. Straight
spine. Stout his neck's pedestal of head and handspan brow.
                                                        Black hair.
Dark seaweed lashes fringe sapphire blue eyes glint light humour
warmly, glance from under that flop hat his job done on his kerb
                                                        squat.
Strong nose. Square chin. Slight his smile of marble-white teeth
                                                        in sensual
mouth. Amidships, port and starboard, bristle broad, care-curled
proud moustaches signal his heart's humours, nickname. He's our
                                                        personal
bar's bootblack. No black Egyptian he but Alex' old-stock world.

He knows all we midday regulars one to one respectfully and our
daily bartalk's bait and badger, thrust and parry without quarter.
He takes our shoes as taken, in silence shines their shapes as for
contenders until our noonday thirst's well slaked.
He boxes his own corner.

He doesn't drink or talk himself nor take any side in our discourse
of world events. His moustaches tack and gybe their own safe course.

II

After my long absence, thirteen years,
I return unannounced, that long older.
My first call's at Pastroudis to look for
those friends used, at midday, on high chairs,
sit to the bar for our aperitif.
We kept our bills in one glass on the shelf.

I find Pastroudis and its people changed.
The bar's gone. Gutted. My friends too gone
elsewhere or dead. I stand awry on my own
in a coffee-and-cakes place, confused, estranged.
The customers today sit pairs in love
and retired couples who don't speak or move.

Then, there, asquat on the kerb, I recognise
that form and face. He's shining shoes. *Moustaches!*
He's dressed the same, flop hat, winter galoshes.
He's seen and knows me too I realise
and when our eyes meet he salaams a hand
to head, slight-smiles sadly, shrugs the end.

I take a chair to him and place my foot
on his old box. He takes my new shoes off,
places his pavement mat. That's not enough.
He proffers a cigarette from under his hat
out of his ear. His spine's bent. His hair's
grey, his teeth amber. One dead eye stares.

Neither of us comments on our lives or
change. Silence speaks its own soliloquies.
He's welcomed me as one from the old days
who left for work elsewhere but now sits here
again. My new shoes shone, he tips his moustache.
I reach to pay. He whispers one word: *Malesh.*
"Never mind. It doesn't matter."

Alexandria Elegy

Your glance last night took me back to our while together
on that bed we call our Mediterranean.

You hav e seen so much worth and dross wash up to your
shore with each slow change on the winds of time.

When this sailor shipped in to you, searching for all
might give him safe anchorage on life's voyage,

he took you as he found you: bypassed but still lovely,
tied to no one but your glorious past.

Languor in an older, well bred woman challenges
her chosen man to shape a life for both.

She may inspire some new play from each day's tired text
will cast those parts gone dull in live, fresh roles.

Of noble lineage, to me you played that part
and locked it in your deceptive shades of

autumn, darks of winter when we burned late night candles
in hideouts of imagination's fantasy.

Then you took my every vocal entrance or silent exit
with feigned interest, in comic or tragic pose.

Sweet spring. Then summer's white light brought distracting
                                                          fashions
with large sunhats that hid your age's old features.

With time those seasons' comedy lose their strained free laughter
so's not to end in tragedy's betrayal.

That's when it's time to pack and move life's show elsewhere.
I did just that and left with one slow wave.

Goodbye Alexandria

When we met your mature face enthralled me.
Your look, the map of wisdom's labyrinthine
invitation we knew could engulf me.
Your midnight eyes' glance shone my naïve love's ruin.
Yet what lay hidden in your silent mind
seduced me in to search, in hope to find.

Illi shuftu. The things that I have seen
show all I need to learn for now, dear friend.
The love envisioned, that slowly might have been
consummated as the life of my fond
fantasy, tired to the routinely dull.
We exhausted marriage in our betrothal.

My human penchant for an older woman
gave me to you wardrobed in four cultures.
Your face changed with the year's each due season
while we indulged our appetites like epicures.
With time, dropped masks, facades revealed your age
so that my heart's now turned away from marriage.

Too restless for that end, I must confess
your jaded ways no longer raise my fancy,
spell out the end of love's exhausted converse.
The sirens of new ports sing sweetly to me.
Here I am dying, Alex, dying. My hour
has come to sail. Tomorrow I weigh anchor.

A Winter Night

Left to themselves they play backgammon by the silent fire,
throw their hesitant dice's whisper to and from each other. Shuffle
of their separate black and red counters: church and state,
spirit and mind, emotion and body, woman and man.
Syllables of query, doubt, consent, satisfaction. Swish of dice.
One plays northern style, the other southern. An engaging challenge.

I sit elsewhere, a wanderer in the tent of my imagination,
smoking, sipping, scribbling these lines. Time attenuates life.
Life and death seem two foolscap sheets of paper spread open
between which we lie, and lay black on white in script.

The southerly wind that softens the stiffness of this season
makes welcome this morning's fresh beginning. That birds' song
in our nearby churchyard has stopped. The moon hides in its wood.
The dice's last tumble done, the game's triangles fold a rectangle.
I succumb to sleep as a nomad curls up beside his camel.

The Poet C.P. Cavafy's Mother

Alexandrian evening. Polite promenade.
Fresh northwester off your Euclidic Corniche.

At home upstairs, off Ramleh Square,
your mother, in lace, claws on to you dressed
upright in dark suit, starched white collars,
hide-behind pince-nez. She slouches to bed at ten.

My mother, *Feathereye*, with a gesture would say
"Take this money. Keep up your end of the night."
She departed in angel blue for her hereafter
unlike your Haricleia, your family horror too.

Then, sure she's asleep, you're off to the Attarine area
deserting the library of your frustrated imagination.

The reality of experience, imagined or lived,
generates the life of what we leave after us.

Joseph Brodsky Visits

In the early summer of eighty-eight
You came in on the New York morning flight
And sauntered nonchalantly through our town,
Our life—like a sailor coming home

From sea. We welcomed you like some prodigal
We'd awaited for many years. In ritual
The whole town came to see and hear you, even
Though most didn't know yet you were Russian

Jewish by way of old St. Petersburg
But now live in Greenwich Village, New York.
They asked me what to say to such an exile
In our small, historic harbour of Kinsale.

That's what you and I share between us:
The secret sores of prodigal perseverance,
Our exiled souls' new scars. The more fortunate,
I've reclaimed my homeland. You're still expatriate.

Each form of exile grants favour and disfavour:
It gives detachment from all that's familiar,
Perspective on old icons of childhood and growth,
A keener view of what plays false, what truth.

It extends the borders of new awareness
In such realms as self-doubt, self-value, aloneness
And strengthens our sense of purpose, focuses insight
Which puts its stamp on all's attempted, done right.

Our prodigality serves up its worthwhile
Riches, it sensibly banks the beneficial
Wealth of experience: depart, confront, return
Equipped to bear the weight of our human burden.

The Painter Gisèle

Today dawns the four square year of your glorious age.
At eighty you have witnessed our century's start.
We're sure you'll live to see this millennium out.
In what, perhaps, has passed as man's most savage
and most expansive century—two world wars,
the atom split, cubism, man on the moon –
you've been blessed with the vocation that's art's
to practise for life among your loving and loved.

We who celebrate you today do so
aware sacrifice made art for life,
life for art in times of love and war,
of aspiration, distress, consummation.
"To do instead of not doing. . . the rest is dross."
Doing makes life, undoes death.

Life is short.
Art lasts long.

Each of life's seasons
yields its own harvest.

I

The innocence of childhood anthologises
those images of people, places, paraphernalia age
recognises in grandchildren who repeat the cycle
in summer sunshine, by winter fireside:
Gigantic presences of elders in rooms or gardens,
town or country. Those objects inherited from elders
we, when elders, will pass down. Icons carry memory on.

II

The hot blood of youth in its confused dare-devil love
dances round the so-called "bait of evil" and its vision
of a future in adventure, profession, vocation: first friends,
challenges, victories, defeats, healed wounds, broader horizons.
Early death in sickness or action. Separation from the familiar.
The process of love. Affirmation. Marriage. Parenthood.
Aspiration to live to a ripe old age without complaint.

III

The gravity of the prime of life without its masks and methods.
Encounters with a past has survived to the present. Re-evaluation.
Realization. Disillusion. "Nepotism is not always blind".
Affirmation in full maturity. Its magnanimity or madness.
All that resists old age accumulates plans to compensate
for its deficiencies. Defences manned as against disease:
regularity, routine, creative imagination advantage to the end.

IV

Mellow old age can comfort and delight at the end
of life's struggles and storms. To fault age is a fault
of character not of age. The disciplined—those with inner resources
for living the good life—find old age a pleasure and see
only good in Nature's Law. There peace and serenity end
life morally well lived with grace in good taste. An honourable estate.
Death ends or begins all. Either end leaves nothing to mortally fear.

*

All passion spent the mind's free to follow its own bent.
We may live out our enthusiasms of thought, reason, deliberation.
Age stimulates resistance, must stand up for its rights, refuse
any sell-out to anyone, maintain its station's seniority to the end.
Then we won't notice age's process. Time lives on after life dies.
When we've had our fill of all engaged our interest we've had
our fill of our life's fullness—then sense our time to leave.

Keep a constant interest in the parts we play. The last act
demands and rewards the most for the true actor.
We may not leave the stage until directed to by Nature
so we must applaud the comedy that's Death or else go mad.
Nature writes its proper *finale* for life's natural drama.

The wise exit life with equanimity and no wish to replay it.
Chant no dirge for death.
Sing joy.

September 1992

Italy

Village

Today
let us toast their festivals
with joyful smiles in the cafés
across the Italian diaspora.

Today
the villages
marry life
around the world.

Today
in this village
the mothers in their parish
run up and down
with the *pizzelle* of the feast day.

Today
let us toast
the Pescolani.
Proud of their ancient tradition
they stand upright.
Their young companions
have left home
on a one-way ticket
and their hopes.

Go and multiply in happiness.

Today
we wish you to give the world
beautiful village children.

Town

The laughter of churchbells wakes
that silence was last night's sleep.
They welcome who rises and takes
strength from another day's deep
blue sky crowning the country.

A high surround of mountains
piazzas this town on its hill,
whose houses necklace the town's
square—a fountain its navel.
My outside staircase nobly

leads to a convent, now empty,
with its walled window niches.
A millennium of history
in these streets' neat stitches
backgrounds their human comedy.

Children in school uniform
brandishing life's schoolbags
chatter their way in uniform
to class. Their parents have jobs.
At this height life is stately.

City

The noble head of ancient Parma city
poises proudly on the shoulder of her
country's body. Celtic promiscuity
conceived her. Reared Roman. Papal later
she's bred dynasties of all human art.
We enjoy them now in her every part,
as she stretches beside the river Po.

Her story graces education to all
who heed: Do what you will because you know
you may produce a creature of your will.
Once done, all that follows will enhance
your art of life, your final, mortal dance.

The seven mouths of its amber river's band
makes this town one lake-house on rich farmland.

Her Birthday Night
for Florence Tamburro

Tonight, my love, you sleep far away on our island and I
imagine the air, still for lack of wind off the sea, and you,
as that ageless star which attends your waning moon
on the serene mountain that gazes across the choral waves.
Boats cradle at anchor in the harbour, the couples in their homes.
Tonight my fantasy conjures your birthday celebrations
as we used to celebrate it together, year after loving year.

All day the compliments of friends and, in their traditional way,
elders congratulate you while they happily recall times past.
The young with gaiety evoke your promise of a happy future.

Evening preparations for the night's festivities. After dark
the gathering of all at hospitable tables to wine and dine you.
Toasts to love and a long life. They chant: 'Eat and drink well,
sleep easy at night and, when you feel like it, get married.' Then
music for traditional dances we used to dance together in love.

Tonight who leads you to the floor, my lady? Who matches
your stance and pose, step and pause, glance and glide
with that heel and toe footwork bespeaks courtship's admiration?
Whose raised arms' spin and wheel provokes you proudly aloof,
trembles your heart's elation, contains your feigned evasion, my dear?

Next you step out with all your friends to that graceful 'present
then pass' in choral harmony, with natural pleasure in movement.
The innocent play, physical talk, ingenuous art of the dance
that woos and wins all hearts to love and joy in life together.

My dance died forever when you renounced me after our last
summer there. Since then my once ballet of life around you
now shuffles by, day after solitary day, to its stamped stop.

Tonight, out of view of you, this scribble on the page is my dance
alone with you in fantasy, and also with our friends, since departed.

Your birthday night, now gone silent, traces those star-crossed
paths of lovers who straggle adoringly back to the village. The empty
alleys look like your necklace dropped on the floor undressing.
An occasional light shines on a balcony for all of you. Memories.
Everything that reminds me of you goes through me like a spear.

Now you sleep in your quiet rooms. What faded hopes, fresh
fantasies play music and dance to it in your dreams tonight?
Do you think of me now as wearing a willow flower daily?
So much time unlived together since you left our blessed
yet cursed lives in this ghetto we call the human affair.

Midnight. That crow in the graveyard of my heart
caws. Your personal day we each remember yearly
has passed. This scrawl that speaks my life lingers
like a phone voice fading but audible.
Slave to your unwearying voice
I rest now, confined with
ever the singer you.

after Giacomo Leopardi 1788-1837

May Day

After spring labour today's the first of summer
with hope of new life that will hold for good.
Last night we erected and dressed up the whitethorn,
drank and sang, danced round the roaring bonfire.

Some slunk away to lark in secret bushes.
A few heard cuckoos coo love and forgot
you must not give anything away May Eve.
Do and they'll take all of worth you possess.

At dawn we washed our faces in May Day dew.
That beautifies. Yet we must remember
not to wed in May. That might prove bad luck.
That's why we dress all month in our work clothes.

These are customs long dead in town they say.
Now all will change. New ways begin today.

Horse
for Gisèle O'Grady

Thoroughbred hands high, combed down
tail trails straw. Stunted stub
strength of thoroughbred tail's root.
Prong eared, sloe eyed elegance,
silent with horse sense, crotchety
as a Celtic goddess looking filly eyed
at me looking. Muscled neck strength knotted.
Careful carve of fetlock, of knuckle
at knees' knob, broad shoulder blades
forward as man's chest.
Spine's supple curve,
like a gnomic line,
conducts imagination.
Haunches hand shaped as sculpture,
hoofs planted hatchets, forelegs
definite as dolmens.
Nostrils those mimetic
voids known in nature.
Lips mobile as wavelets.
Highhatched eyesocket.
A broad handspan that forehead,
triangle starred the target centre.
Straight as a forearm the face bone
from muzzle to forelock.
Belly a craftily coopered barrel.
One quick hind hoof kick
could kill. Watch for that.

Crosstalk

What's writ today in verse?
One nought, I must confess.

Nothing? After weeks of woesome weather
our sky cleared, the sun shone bright.
Yet you made nought. With high temperature
you always sit at home and write.

That was my plan this morning too
but my head turned askew, my vision awry.
I couldn't help it. I'm human like you.
Despite best intentions today died without epiphany.

We know your pledge to do what must be done.
Our weather favoured you. You'd no promise
to others; rose free of worries. Summer's season
over, all distractions gone. What's your excuse?

My day began normally, with a determined plan:
Return to routine! Sit down to work! Be strong!
With purpose I sat to table, new paper with raised pen.
You're a demon for discipline. What went wrong?

The out of mind caught my eye, bent me
up against my awareness. I didn't expect it so,
thought all that behind me now leaving me, us free
to write gamesome as a fiddler in flight, elbows akimbo.

The unforeseen factor? At this time of life and year
when nought happens that we may have to confess?
That expects explanation. You have wrought your career,
your time's your own or God's. Your only enemy laziness.

You know what my life's like here. No one to talk
to on my own. No companion, no family, except
perhaps the schoolteacher's dog takes me for a walk
and the crows that tell me to sleep, assure I've not overslept.

Weekly I plod down to the shop in town for groceries,
regularly I like to go out in the garden to turn my bicycle.
Nightly there's no voice in the house except the grosseries
of the last World News, which is not what we'd call musical.

That's how today began. The hound died of heart muddle
at my feet under the desk some time ago. I shaved for town,
then all in order, like the postman with his foot on the pedal
of his bicycle, I took the Low Road, talking to the dog. Common.

The sun shone bright in a sky swept clean of cloud,
the woods about me wove green through green on brown.
The birds' excited converse sounded like society abroad
chatting at an international garden party. Wonderful.

Emergence on to the main road presented me with my local
tavern just opened. The Muse wears many guises of temptation.
A brief stop to glance today's paper over one refreshing gargle,
then on to shop and get back home for lunch. That's human.

Between the newspaper, local parley and the glass for glass
all my shopping money flowed salubriously down the drain.
Now home my belly growls hungry, my pocket feels penniless.
The tavern's the cape of no hope. Back home I couldn't write a line.

Autumn Festival

After our August celebrations
that farmer began his harvest.
Example, with its stipulations:
survey work done, save what's best.

This month, when my next birthday dawns,
I hope to score nine times seven
years old. One more septet remains
of our human three score and ten

to give final form to my life
and what is mine to leave. Then exit,
with old age's sigh of relief,
standing by what has been well weft.

Now, as they die I cross out friends'
addresses. Beside them I read some
that may not stay much more. Who ends
the last must silence on alone.

And yet, just now I drank a beer
with one old pal who today had,
fifty seven years past, with dear
good luck, survived at sea torpedoed.

He doesn't tug up his bed sheets, yet.
The day we start that means death's close.
This hare still hops ahead of that
mower, to the hag-sheaf's magic trance.

Michael Hartnett 1941-1999

I

Two dinghies
on life's seas
we met in that anchorage
of McDaid's pub, Dublin,
among the ships of our time. Many
of them have sunk since then.

Plebs and poets admire you.
The red lights of our capitol tempt you.
You succumb and find imagination
as dangerous as the drowning ocean.
Yet you swim on, stay afloat
on those tousled sheets of the poet.

Your books of poems spoke to me on my boat.
Still, your tide did flow in to drown you.
Your poem I brought to read, as they sank you
in your grave, went lost overboard on my way:
"has gone today who was once beside me."
Wherever our sailor kind voyage, we sail alone.

II

We praise your youthful vision in your village
of childhood and your fluency in the tongues
our people speak. Both voice your poets' language
in songs and laments of life's joys and wrongs.

Elders protected you as their rare child,
thereafter you sprout, bloom and blossom your names.

Our island towns and cities and lands beyond
became forums for your published poems.
You sang with true faith in your Muse and she
blessed your devotion. The lives and deaths of friends
set Fate's example. Your stitches you cobbled in words
like stones on the road you took through life's mystery.

The village craves the city, indulges and gets
crocked. So did human you. The poet survives.

Dream

The delta that wombs Alexandria? The hills that bosom
Tuscan shores? A Greek island? Either way familiar
to me, if unrecognisable. Our maternal Mediterranean.
A house, indoors. Somebody's spacious villa. Various
stepped planes of flagstone floors; walls, arches, stairs
in shades of white with dark wood stripes at angles.
Sparse furniture save for two rectangular trunks,
divans, a long table. Paintings hang in chosen perspectives
under high ceilings, ochre timbers and extended spaces
at different levels. Niches with statuettes, the black comma
of a grand piano on a raised floor. Beside it reclines
a shapely cello. She stands between them, facing me.
Her rich black hair tumbles down the sides of her
well-appointed features on to her shoulders. As I do,
she wears a rectilinear linen tunic roped at slender
hips. It falls to her bare feet like a religious habit or
ancient Greek or Roman gown. Behind her, at angles,
two open spaces give views on vineyards, olive groves
overlook a tranquil green sea, blue sky, white light.
Out there a boy's voice calls to me desperately, in silence.
He too wears a tunic. His tearful lament traumatises.
In the vineyard a monklike old man continues pruning,
waits to assist whoever will move to the youth's distress.
The silent cello, mute piano, watchful paintings, statues;
the sunlit tranquillity of all nature's surround focus
these incomparable pleas of that painted human voice.

Olga Jwaideh O'Grady 1930-2000

From girlhood you grow classical woman
who loves culture, fine art. Both, born, grew up
as you in Iraq's Garden of Eden.
Adult, you tour traditional Europe.

Romantic, you choose Paris for mature
studies, there make an act of faith in life
well lived with mind and heart to face down grief.
Love and good humour breed well together.

Because for you he vows the finest art
the poet icons above all other.
With him you dance the music of your heart
which creates a poem between you forever.

Travels in our maturation enrich our growth's aspiration,
yet mere distractions tire with time and we wish to create anew.
You find the Garden of Europe through Rome where all cultures renew
but choose to live in some London you aspired to in childhood vision.

That day dawns for us all when we decide, accept the where and how
we shall live our decline through age till nature makes her decision.
All settle then for time and space, echo ancestral tradition
which most revolt against when young, to tailor our own tomorrow.

You bear and raise our fine daughter. She prides us now with her children
in that world where you exampled classical imagination.
You left our lives casually, unaware it was your last exit.
Where you smile now you know whom you loved won't forget.

Self Portrait

I

My garden, high hedged from public
view in decades of neglect, lives
its natural life through my lack
of interest in a world that grieves.
In my suspended imagination
that outside world's some other person.

My garden's converse, while green
in season, springs flashes of flower,
nettles too that sting intruded on.
All weeds go wild in hot summer
but this proud parasite will thorn
your heedless gesture, let me warn.

The provocative pose and fetch
of that orchid, like lies, repel.
Now it smiles the grimace a witch
shows when she casts her evil spell.
The petals of favourite roses wither
as once sweet words now turn bitter.

Those pigeons voice their round vowel hoot,
like monks chant, from our churchyard trees
in antiphon to those more throat
cacophonic crows and magpies.
Each year birds nest in my rafters
and stain my walls inside like cancers.

Of my flanking neighbours in their
nineties one dozed off dead at home.
The one left lives old age with vigour.

That's what matters, all tried or done:
live life aware, curious, involved,
die gladly, like an equation solved.

When our pub's old men die we notch
them down. Their yarns live on their while.
The young move up to take their watch
and steer pub talk in their new style.
We all enjoy our glass and chatter
but can't, alas, do so forever.

The master of the children's school
retired this year. He brought up three
generations; knows each child still.
Those here gave him his last hurray,
those gone live round the classroom globe
he let them turn as teaching bribe.

Beyond lies the city, mascarad whore,
its children blind to local history.
Ancient ruins decay, like the poor
left to die in conditional misery.
The lives of most embarrass in want,
apathy, ignorance, middleclass cant.

There lie the curtain-hidden ravages
of dried up spinsters, withered bachelors,
couples childless in planned marriages,
chatterbox widows, silent widowers.
The young survive in blocked cement
on bad TV, unemployment.

Reject the world of rubbish I thought,
care for that garden of your soul.
One's life is mundanely sold and bought;
save time to elevate life's goal.

Balance between public, private;
give love its foremost place, live it.

One's day should have simple routine:
physical, mental; sleep, calm dream.
The functions of this old machine
that's to me work in regular time.
The rest's awareness, curiosity,
imagination's live fantasy.

II

This cottage, dubbed my hermitage,
stands built long past with local stone.
These rooms once housed the vicarage
of our locked church which now serves none.
These walls inside were plastered white,
rising damp blackened them like blight.

My furniture, good hand-me-downs,
serves its purpose like traditions.
Bookshelves contain my life's concerns
in literature and our abrasions.
Everywhere hangs a photograph
of friends, now dead or more than half.

On window sill boat lamps to port
and starboard. 'Midships a model Brendan
the Navigator's boat at heart
recalls voyages I've half forgotten.
Seashells, glass buoys, dog's bleached backbone,
that stuffed bird in flight on her own.

On this carpenter made desk, left
to me by an ageing painter,

stand *mementi mori*: hand craft
and art of times once lived elsewhere.
A life reduced now to this goat's
skull that grins at wine glass, cigarettes,

outlived reading glasses, fountain
pens, dead diaries, old false teeth,
my reader's lectern. From Pound, old then,
his ink-stand: a master's gift to student.
That tortoise ashtray from my son
reminds he's married, fathered, gone.

On my bedroom walls hang pictures
of time lived on a Greek island.
Paintings by friends. Their mixture
creates nostalgic states of mind.
Family photos hang indications
of five nomadic generations.

On my bedroom window shelf stands
an ancient Greek piece for eyedrop
or tear—you choose between your hands.
Half my finger high its round top
circles our European culture
and my personal infrastructure.

My mute wardrobe of lifeless clothes
(too foreign here, or out of fashion)
recalls seasons, climates, weathers
elsewhere, reflects that generation
before mine and the travel spoils
of an influential uncle's

sea cruises in search of love, self
or both—then shipped home still alone.

Does that trait run in the male half
only? Most females seem prone
to stay home and raise family,
then watch sons grow to take off early.

One day after a sound night's sleep
I rose at noon and stood a moment
at pause in thought. Sudden sharp deep
pain like electric light flashes on joint
of spine and pelvis. I buckle double.
Agony. Straighten. Now I hobble.

Male and female vertebrae disjoint
when ageing too. That certain nerve
which worms between their juncture won't
take stress. Pain shoots and kills one's verve.
A measured flow of good red wine
at night in bed helps ease my pain.

A wisdom tooth complains. Dentists
opine my mouth suffers neglect,
save what may serve their denturists
to make new teeth will read correct.
Although your mouth's away, put on
a new face with each new expression.

The hair thins on the scalp that crowns
my head. Eyelashes look schismic,
eyes bilingual, this nose a clown's.
Ears tune well or ill to music,
accent. Mouth narrows from silence.
My tongue's gourmet; its talk of substance.

One day I woke, my left eye blind,
then next my left hand lost its hold
and my left leg dragged behind,

I'm not so active as of old
which keeps me home more than I like.
Bad balance won't allow a bike.

Cobwebs woven on walls, everything—
like family history—remains left
untouched for decades. They will bring
good luck it's said. They manuscript
their tale of all nomadic life.
Each web recalls a child or wife.

Some friends call occasionally
to check if I am still alive.
That's good fellowship, neighbourly.
What more need one expect? I'm safe
against the plight of being just left
to rot in bed, on floor, bereft.

One day I'll see the rats slink in
and stay, because I can't crawl out
of bed or just don't give a damn.
That happened one I loved. He quit
all fight, all talk, all food. That's when
I'll pull the sheet eyes high, give in.

Seasons

It's not this time of year at all.
Spring lies inert, abused by weather;
life's seasonal renewal won't cohere
and summer hopes don't flower poetical.

Midlife's confusion knots the same
when nature's urgencies in spring
encourage live adventure. Love on the wing,
grounded by age, can rise no more for shame.

Winter mopes on in silent sloth
until the promise that's spring's humour
will arouse for, then indulge summer
passion. Autumn gifts repose to both.

Seasons that once encouraged flight
now make a joke of their prerequisite.

The Battle of Kinsale 1601
for John V. Kelleher

On the twenty first day of September
sixteen hundred and one,
the last Spanish armada sails over
Kinsale's safe port's horizon.

They bring four thousand armed soldiers
from Europe and Africa
and sixteen hundred horse saddles
to seat a cavalry.

Del Aquila their general
alights on our short quay.
His dark faced captains in a circle
stand round for all to see.

His dark skin sailors from the Azores,
Africa wear earrings,
colourful turbans. They raise long oars
in their naval salutings.

That night they crowd Kinsale's taverns
after their voyage from Spain.
They stack their armour high as squadrons
and toast far-off Lisbon.

In foul October weather Mountjoy
surrounds Kinsale harbour.
From Brown's Mills camp he can survey
his enemy on the shore.

Their ships now gone back home the Spanish
soldiers get housed in town.

They will live well here on the Irish
until O'Neill gets down.

Weather turns the worst in memory.
Endless cold rain floods all
the English trenches in muddy misery.
Each day they live in hell.

Most die of cold and exposure.
Well housed in town and fort
each Spaniard is a trained fighter.
Attack. Defend. Retreat.

In torrential rain Mountjoy
assaults Rincurran Castle.
The Irish-Spanish defence goes bloody
and England wins that scuffle.

Ten weeks after the Spaniards' arrival
O'Neill and O'Donnell march down
to join Aquila at Kinsale,
surround England between them.

They confront Mountjoy and Carew.
While constant rain floods field
and bog, the men both sides freeze through
in this winter's killing cold.

Mountjoy's ten thousand strong. His ten
gunships shell Castle Park.
After five days the beaten
Spaniards surrender, talk.

England's guns bombard Kinsale town.
Del Aquila resists
surrender, for Christ and Spain.
For now Mountjoy desists.

No food for Mountjoy's men and horse,
they now desert. O'Neill
closes tighter. The wind blows harsh
rain and cold for all.

The Spanish and Irish food is gone,
they now eat cats and dogs.
In winter's ice cold wind and rain
they die like exposed hogs.

Within a mile of Mountjoy's men
Tyrone and Tyrconnell,
bogged down by thunderstorms of rain,
disagree on battle.

Del Aquila and O'Donnell
want to attack that night.
He's held back so long now O'Neill
thinks it's too soon to fight.

In quiet Kinsale the Spaniards wait
for some Irish signal.
None comes. Unknown country and night
cut off and lose O'Donnell.

The worst of bad weather breaks down
Irish-Spanish contact.
With no cavalry O'Neill crawls on
to join the expectant

Spaniards. At dawn's first light he faces
the full power of English
horse and foot. He about faces.
Reconnoitre. Patience.

Too late. The English front attacks.
More than three thousand men.
O'Neill holds ground. More horse impacts.
The Irish get cut down.

The situation in their favour
Ireland should have sat tight.
O'Neill decided against his nature.
He lost in an hour. Fate.

That Christmas Eve he wrote
the fatal page of Ireland's
history and of her heroes' spirit.
They're destroyed by England's.

O'Donnell and remaining Spanish
sail out to Spain. There jail
awaits Don Juan's disgrace. An English
agent poisons O'Donnell.

O'Neill retreats three hundred miles
on foot to his north's winter.
Rejected now by all, he exiles
to Rome, sickens, dies there.

That day's defeat decided Tyrone's
and Ireland's future history.
This war more than any other ones
killed Celtic memory.

Had they stayed faithful unto Time,
as Time had unto them,
they would not have brought their true own
selves and Ireland to ruin.

Voices
to the Painter Gisèle, for Her Ninetieth Birthday

Your vine of life fruits full again this year
and vintages your best to share with us.
We'll taste and feast on your ripe memories
of past times and lives lived as time's guest.

At first light your birthday will dawn and shine
all day for you. All you love will radiate
response in kind. The stitch in time of your
first decade saved your ninth decade to knot.

In childhood we gather life's images
round us: places, people, those things that catch
our attention, please or displease all, as
they may do thereafter when they repeat.

In youth's dreams of adventures in new ways
of life we dare to broaden our horizon.
We work in happy hope through hurt and heal
to shape life in profession, vocation.

To live our love of life defeats mere death.
All live, all die one way or another.
What we make that outshines our mortality–
children, lives for others, art-examples.

Human history effects all life in peace,
through war. What we make well helps growth improve.
All love helps heart and soul survive through strife,
inspires each joyful flight of peace's dove.

The peak of life, when real, rejects all masks,
stands clear as truth. It may revive old-time
values to live the age process with strength,
enliven each day's order with fantasy.

Ageing matures, mellows our stress from struggle
and those who order time to live life well
find joy in age, comfort in nature's law.
Age's serenity transcends all that is mortal.

My School English Teacher
for Thomas P. Cole, 1892-1964

The first day you swing in to our classroom
for our English literature lesson
we do not know you from our years before.
Senior teacher status kept your person
at that remove. As of today we're yours
till our remove grants us senior status
as grownups in life's university.
From now on life's what you make out of us.

We boys rise with respect when you enter
on your stroll to our room's rostrum. You hold
two tomes against your chest, your coat of arms.
My pair lie on my desk, brandnew, unread.
When we sit down your scan punctuates us.
You lift one volume in each hand, declare:
"Poetry! Prose. Today we'll read a poem!"
I had seen no teacher like you before.

You stand six straight feet tall and lean. Your head's
poise makes you a reversed exclamation
mark to that word: Poem! Then you Euclid
arms, hands, fingers to inscribe the word's sound
on blank blackboard as four sacred letters.
You tell your script "poets live responsible
to we readers for every word they write.
If they do not they are not forgivable."

Book in left hand you read aloud with calm,
right hand conducts the rhythm as in music.
"What does the poet say to us?" you ask
then have us read aloud to your tick tock.
When we work out, write down the poet's theme

you point out his technique. That you call form.
"Words paint pictures. Vowels and consonants,
rhymes and pauses music each line's rhythm."

Bell! You wipe your sole word off blackboard's face.
"Find out all you can on that poet's life,"
sings your last line as you jaunt your exit.
Your presence dawns my future mode of life.
Libraries become Aladdin's cave
of lives: poets, artists, great musicians.
How they lived. My states of mind now warn me:
create each day with no complications.

When next we face the same poem, you face
our blank blackboard, scribe your next proper noun:
Poet! You ask "What's that phenomenon?"
We think, outside school no one like that is known,
say: "We study their poems for exams.
We only know about famous sportsmen."
You nod: "Play your sports well to win the games.
Poets play life's games and score with their poems."

Once we can write on a poem's theme, technique
your comments focus on what you deem rare.
My awareness grabs some, catches others
as your eccentric language starts to read real.
You mention writers, artists, composers
we should be aware of outside our course
then, off the cuff, why they're so important
and spell out their curious names for us.

Down from tuneless rafters, through blind walls you
inscape creation's poems, cubist inselves.
What I hear, see won't *enface* the same again
as I travel free gratis on bookshelves.

Now, as inself cubists my agenbite
of inwit, poems instress Euclidic forms
in selves my whoness shows, or fades
for me to instress art constructs with words.

My ego steals from all life's lives. Thoughts
of their worlds reflect sometimes in my own.
When we do that no one poem's poet
will fade out in our classroom forgotten.
You get life from teaching; I mine from that.
We're both content with what we think, contrive.
Your master's psyche vocations my poet's,
helps create my life and my afterlife.

I hope that cloud you now read on up there
encourages applause for what your one
published schoolboy has put on shelves round here.
When I join you we'll talk forever on
countries where my teaching housed me, poets
admired by you whom I've since met, have known;
how art gets made from life's experience
and, when we make it well, how it lives on.

Friendship

Whatever our forecast on air or screen,
while we can we must love each day for all
it dawns to give us of life or lack to take on
of our world's ways to night's rest from day's work.

The challenge of engagement with relentless time
generates continuity in the face
of mortal process. What we may confirm
may example others in their place.

In sun and storm take joy in sense awareness.
Draw a child's life-smile with each breath of survival:
from the insect's crawl across a road
and ours from crib to kitchen, church or castle
and that inspiring force, motivation.
That brightens dark for all, engine's effort,
lifts up who fall. Life is beauty in manifestation,
fertilizes friendship that survives henceforth.

Old Haunts

After long, felt absence, every return
to old haunts of one's youthful past saddens.
The layout's seldom still the same. The turn
over of new owners and staff deadens
any urge to banter conversation
about old friends, the new state of the nation.

Young cronies of the past, once regulars here
for ritual meetings then, have grown and wed
and gone to work and live their lives elsewhere.
New faces with new values show now instead.
The very taunt and tease, the give and take
of banter too has changed. It all sounds fake.

By chance some ageing regular then turns
up and that may raise a vague, timeless nod
of recognition. Such slight welcome warms
the chill left by those old pals gone abroad,
reassures that the true of the tribe don't forget.
That's silent companionship without regret.

Seachange

From here on my terrace I face the sea.
Morning's mists crawl quietly about me
like camouflaged commandos practising
a silent raid on their objective. Playing
possum at my feet that deaf old dog
seems unaware time does not give or beg.

The world around presents glorious nature,
its various forms a haze of shade and colour
through that sea mist which now envelopes all.
A tractor stammers a start beyond the wall
of my churchyard. That farmer works his farm.
Our mixed lives here know neither hate nor harm.

A songbird trills unseen above my head
in joyful freedom like the unencumbered.
A crow's cacophony quavers in kind:
antiphony in morning's misted mind.
That ocean looks as calm as inland water.
My day's all mine, with neither rein nor halter.

Whale

I am the whale
merlin master of the seas'
mysteries in this ocean
of various high singers
dolphin dancer dazzlers.

I am that lone, maker whale.
My must swims with me, my constant
madonna, Magdalene, Mona Lisa
on my odyssey to the shores of my origins.
I play with sea waves as poems do with lines,
poured bronze with sketches, palette colours of ballet
and trapeze dancers on the canvas of eternity.

When I take my joyous leap alone
I curve the sky's rainbow.
Threatened, I'm that vertical deep
diver who disappears like a druid
in the labyrinthine fathoms of vocation.

My every movement's mime in mine
uniquely and while I hold no grudge
against my fellows, when provoked to strike
I devastate, then continue my perennial,
decided directions forgiving, forgetting detached.
Nothing's random in my turn and tune. Nothing's
chance. All is reason, rational rectitude.

Harpoon hit I dive and hide,
a silhouette beneath the surface
among my fellows. We're a school apart.
So few now we must protect each other
daringly, alternately indifferent to attention.

I am the whale, solitary as an island
in an archipelago of genealogical differences
and distances. With my kind there's little rapport.
Sometimes I swim casually, other times daringly.
My domain spreads the seas of tradition, tidal languages,
I swim with my fellows menaced by marauding humans.
I voyage odysseusly. Those who cling on to
my back never distract my dedicated direction,
drop off with time. I enjoy good swim converse,
song in what interests me. My love is constant
yet at times has caused me sadness for life.

In my time I have witnessed so much senseless slaughter
of my kind, such distracted despair among my friends
because of barbarian butchery. Many have given up,
driven themselves on to the shores of desolation to die alone.
Few in the outside world hear or see such wail and decease.
In this polluted ocean I am the whale, Merlin of life's mysteries.

This Island

Should bridges traverse I'll cross
should love kill I'll live on

I'm not me I'm who made me
should my bird perch I shall sing
if this island floats I'm my sea
should I believe my sea I'll make land

As my own sea
I seek my shore
That calls me out to sea
to find the island that's me

Beached I shall awake anew
on my shore, know I'm my sea

All you boats adrift
wish to be islands like me
to sail the sea of life as boats
that sing in their sails repent in their rigs

We all tack and gybe through time
few find the island in themselves

after Ingeborg Bachmann

Grandson

You open your day, our lives, as the lead actor
his theatre. Welcomed, you're prepared for today's
performance with women's talk, Disrobe. Pose with pleasure,
then don the costume tailored for your new play's
old story and stroll out on your stage that reflects our world.
We play to your gestures, plain or purled.

Your first act's set in spring green garden sunshine
where you delight in the morning's comedy with reclined
waves, held gasps, small smiles. Your orchestration.
The players in your park respond in kind.
A pal, or dog you grant men's talk attention,
but your sight's set on grander satisfaction.

Lunch, like newspapers, serves prescribed plates of talk,
that three course play within the play. You sit
up to and hold the table with each remark.
Eat well, then have something to show for it.
Afternoon, like history, gives pause for reflection
on life's confusion and its safe solution.

Nightfall. Your bath is drawn after you dine
so you may wash away your day's distractions.
Then you both plot. She with her glass of wine,
you with your bottle, like two gay tragedians.
Darkness beds you. Sound sleep brings on those dreams,
nightmares that act out your still small boy's schemes.

Winter in Sevilla
for Donna Marcella Altieri

1

Built on rich flatland marshes of the Guadalquiver valley
this ancient city grew into the garden city of smiles it is today.
Winter's morning cloud broke at Sevilla-blue first light
and woke up auroran chant from my Irish soul's memory.
That tunes my awake awareness to audience the crooned tones
of Sevilla's white doves and their background of webstrummed
and plucked guitar rainfall in dawn's halftone daylight.
The churchbells toll the hour of night's death, birth of day's life.

My awakeness hears the lithe, proudly prancing approach, strong snort,
pass, fade out of this day's first macho stallion and carriage
with accompaniment of harness light metal castanuclas and cimbalos
as they trot and roll to Park and Cathedral and start their day's work.
There the drivers whip their quip chat at each other while they
                                                            hug their horses:
"Where do you think you're going with that old tuneless piano of
                                                             a mare of yours?"
"Getting far away from frustrated old Phoenician farts as the likes
                                                             of yourself!"

2

At my every waking up I listen, give thought to
the languages and dialects of all conversing birds.
Then I work at enticing their every enunciation
into verbal notation on my score book to make poems.
That encourages my fantasy to fly about the gardens
of imagination and register the arias of our human operas.

Morning into afternoon we each
face, choose our people round town,
wave to or talk with each other
de paso and spice gossip until
personal duties and evening's arrival
decide, settle our social intercourse.

For others it's time for thoughts
of self and related affairs
with some glances to distraction
from behind shuttered windows
at square, avenue, park, river
and imagined ways of life outside.

At pause to consider my life's
morning progress I hear the city's doves
croon socially under our house eaves,
on window terraces, for human attention,
observe pigeons who desert their coastal
caves for the arches of high city buildings.

My marshes of memory
fertilize winter flowers
in my garden of imagination,
spout the fountains' leap and fall,
fill and enliven fish pools, duck ponds,
rivers with the gallivant of nature's affairs.

Each roused memory of reality
in its own place and time
evokes comparison, evaluation, acceptance
or rejection the better to understand
places, people and paraphernalia of all
reminders of oneself's past and present.

Friends at Funerals

Talking to one good friend of youth this week
brought thoughts of our friends who no longer speak
amongst us; friends who've died and left us alone
as when we first faced onto the world from home.

We walked in the funeral of an old friend
who fought his battle against cancer, round
by round ten stubborn years, but lost his war.
We two now mourned, sizing up each other.

Later, with funeral drinks, we recited
our list of dead friends. We're that unrequited
age when there's still to do before we call
an end, then turn our faces to the wall.

At our age we recognized the presence
of process in the faces facing at us;
may also sense our own faces out. Mask
fronts mask. How do we see ourselves, we ask.

Ageing Siren Concerto

1

Returned after thirty years of travelled absence
I find her still at home, unwed.
We know ourselves in each other straight. Suspense.
Her house the same, she looks aged.

Round this island new youth's been born, grown up, married.
Her church bell rings wedlock, knells death.
The square's clock struck its hours and halves for young and old
some died, some left to earn their worth.

Her smile strains slowly taut beneath her head's grey hair.
Those sparkless eyes strike two flat notes.
Her features, composed celibacy. What's left there
bears a left-home look at long-left boats.

Her speech has soured. That laugh's lost youth's provocation
from lack of love's male challenge.
Her news the vinegar of the virgin left untaken.
Her words false notes in our exchange.

That body's shapeless now. Those breasts, unsuckled, sagged.
Her childless stomach's bloated such
she now looks that unmoulded mass of the unmarried.
They reared her too high-priced to match.

2

Glimpsed unawares before she starts her day
by this lone sailor just ashore, reveals
a presence unimagined once, far away,
when she entranced with her lullaby eyes.

I see she's ageing live before my fading
eye. It's decades since she first song-smiled young
nomad me to her bed, nurtured my growing.
This time ashore this old seadog won't stay long.

Her now dyed hair, like sundried seaweed, clings
upon her turned head. Shaped like scallops
the ears beneath. Her bared forehead brings
to mind lines on faded yellow manuscripts.

Profiled nose and chin compliment while
her lips, like dried fruit, purse etched with lines.
Those once strong teeth, aged loose, restrain her smile
while saggy throat, loose skinned neck spread vines

of wrinkles to scumbled armpits, each drooped breast.
Those once broad shoulders hunch. Her back's curving.
Her belly's paunched from childbirth, love's dead past.
I'll ship out now. Some new, young siren may sing.

3

In age she's long in the tooth, on the pension stage.
Of working class, so no family wealth
and nothing in the bank, no stocks or shares.
Her medical care is common national health.

Her income's from the social security system,
she travels by local bus wherever she goes.
Her wardrobe's left-overs and charity cast-offs
or leftover wardrobes at funeral homes.

For social life she plays the arty clubs
but only goes for the first-night reception.
There she might meet, among the aging snobs,
some lonely gentleman of wealth and station.

She's spent her life on the fashionable fringes
of the arts, the Schools, the University.
She's had to do with, known some famous people
in theatre, painting, music, poetry.

Less world-wise then, she took a poet
for lover. That we all know is one blind alley.
Poets drink your wages, bed your friends, then leave.
Yet she survived all that ingenuous folly.

Now her old age sings out life's last lament:
with whom will she spend her last years of ageing?
Her children, grown and gone, live far away
with theirs. That's why I hear her love's voice calling.

Hermit and Harlot

This hermit and harlot
had a fling one day.
Said the harlot to the hermit
they told me you were gay.

No, said the scribbler hermit,
my quill's not bent at all.
I got my poet's vocation
in coupled rhymes and all.

I see, said the harlot musing,
as she squeezed his penman's pouch.
You've lined me fourteen times now.
Where did you learn so much?

I studied feminine rhyme
and took a foreign degree.
Retired now to my hermitage
I rhyme, but still scan free.

Time Passes

Born in a place fortunate to avoid
the evil of World War in a period
free of the fog of civil strife, I grew
to manhood in personal peace and saw
the best minds of my generation grow
to stature in State and Church, Arts and Law.

Mother Nature's mist from her timeless sea
enshrouds us all. I feel genetically
that subjective age when we begin
to haze out of daily sight and return
safe to the sea of memory and dreams.
My hours, days pass like deltas of small streams.

My mind now seems enclosed by divergent
flows of thought that bring back all those vagrant
times spent with family and friends since gone
or living where I'll not return again.
When speaking with locals I know we both
connect reminders, like patterns on cloth.

Asleep my dreams confuse the places lived in,
the people known, the languages then spoken.
Sometimes a loved one reappears as young
as then; on waking fades like some lost song.
The rest's routine. Divide the day as when
employed: the practical, meet friends for fun.

Half the twentieth century old and father
of the generation will half another,
I face the mists of my final quarter
and stutter start each day like that tractor,
concerned time's mists will haze my family's landscape
and leave no name on my recorded inscape.

Old Satyr

When piss no longer flows so promptly
as when you'd strut a perky youngster

you stand waiting, childlike old man in hand.
Grandfather patience pitifully

regards your past time's bold performer.
You sigh your age, admit all's fair

in nature's battles or else pretend
all's well, with glances here and there

for distraction. Some say to hum
or sing a flighty tune relieves.

It's surer by a running stream
of water. Then all finds natural flow

like that hymn you haven't sung since
your young voice sang in boys' church choirs.

Song may stop too on one high note
held in angelic after-silence.

Now you're back to scratch, you know.
A pebbley whistle may induce

new life. If not try some lament
which will calm old age's agitation.

Then may come that choral flow
will fill the void and reassure

rather than nature's with reluctance
post piddle dribble down your leg.

Crow and Poet

On the seventh of March murders of crows gang
with much tribal crow caw. Identifications.
Silent next day they collect twigs as poets do lines.
After winter's wait in waste, the need for spring
clean up, throw out, build anew . . . "Thanne longen
folk to go on pilgrimages . . ." And poets gang
their several selves in order, being the fulsome year
of their pilgrimage to build their poems for the Muse.

When my crow caws the hour for my last pilgrimage
will call the time to put the twigs of my lives and lines
in order to speak and sing my truth as human poet.

Love

One element of human nature
Never dies, but enlivens, or materializes.
Active, its presence grows mature;
Dormant, its absence ages, withers.

At first encounter illegible,
It takes detached study to decipher.
Well translated it can reveal
A life unknown to its reader.

Like recurrent good health, or ill,
Its energy generates strong life force,
Its lethargy spreads what's lethal.
Withdrawn, its absence breeds unhappiness.

Its script signifies, spells out ability.
The text, complete or related fragments,
Reveals its singular message: harmony.
To pass it by unread shows ignorance.

My Muse

As we grow older she helps me grow younger
In spirit so that, caught unawares
Today, her smile naturally reflects her
Photo, aged seven, on my wall for years.

Where did she bloom from, then or now,
To rule my soul, inspire my mind
From youth to age? I never know
How she'll present herself in kind.

She shows presence as she will:
In objects, thoughts, what passes by.
At times she smiles. Mostly she's still.
Her radiance blinds my souls' wide eye.

Should she frown, her music changes
Tone and tempo. Her phrasing's strong.
Should she scowl, drums and triangles
Requiem her end to love and song.

She shines and fades to no known law,
But when present she conducts
The poetry of love's orchestra.
These days she's here. Her grace still works.

Lady Raffaella

Met in reborn
dolce vita
she tells me Etruscans and Celts
migrated west from Asia about the same time,
met and loved each other in Italy
where they taught those early Romans
how to organise themselves,
create city states.

She takes me to see her Tuscan home
for their autumn wine festival,
exemplifies how to live
her Etruscan lifestyle with joy.
She is of the aristocracy:
in public culturally, in private as family.

These families keep their country homes,
vineyards, olive groves, gardens
for Tuscany's seasonal holidays.
Their city houses and lives
facilitate practical matters,
their children's education
and urban cultural activity.
In public they meet, in private invite
the best national and foreign minds
for companionable conversation
over gourmet cuisine.

They dine and wine well,
sleep easy at night
and when elevated may epiphanise.

In all their twelve Etruscan cities
and crossbred Rome
my lady Raffaella lives without like
in her beauty of mind and body,
refinement of taste and grace,
natural pleasure in the arts of life.

Lovingly awake to our new life
we bathe in the volcanic baths
of her Tuscan countryside,
refresh in iron water springs
rinse our hair in fresh beer
drench our bodies
with last night's rain water
plan our day.

No facial decoration
except when occasion expects
family gold, silver, beads,
each piece naturally quiet.

Her personal concerns focus on the survival
of the student young, maturing artistic, cultured aged
to help create their futures and ends.
Her example inspires vitality in me.

View

My view of half the globe due west from here?
A question mark of land and sea, sunrise
to sunset. That's our coastline's Old Head flasher
beyond! Far, far. Exclamation mark of

Europe's and my full stop before the New
World. There today, my son got up to face
our time's monsters. Young, I took on my few.
With time his will, as mine did, leave their mark.

What may fathers say to sons when they turn
twenty one? Repeat what we were told
by our own? Or confess, with love's concern,
our own mistakes? Tell of the lives of others?

If, from the start, we give silent example
shows life and work, made one by choice, love best,
we may stay quiet. Such marriage grows fruitful.
If we failed this, that's part of our bequest.

New York 2001–Baghdad 2005

His clothes rags on the bones of his body
he brooded over what happened and said:
"I speak what's before my face:
the rivers run dry and sailors
want water to sail their boats on.
The river's course is a sandbank
and the sandbank's piled high against the flood.
The North Wind opposes the South Wind.
Everything good's gone and the land lies prostrate.
Enemies rise in the east and in the west.
And men enter their fortresses. The beasts
of the wild descend to the very doors without fear,
for want of someone to chase them away.
The land runs riot and no one
foresees the outcome—hidden from speech and
sight and hearing. Faces gape blind, confronted
with silence. Men take up weapons of war,
beg for their bread of blood and laugh
with the hysterical laughter of sickness.
I see no one to weep for a death
and man's heart, separated completely
from mourning, seeks selfishly only for self.
People turn their backs while one man
murders another. Sons slaughter their fathers,
brothers each other. Mouths choke with the cry
of 'Love me!' Man holds man in hate
to silence what mouth may speak.
If any man answers, arms rise up
with sticks and the shouts of 'Kill him!'
Nobody knows where midday falls
because the sun casts no shadow.
Silence can only mean repression.

There's much terror abroad and the great
man is a thing of the past in our
time. Quit all laxity, it stares from every face.
Rise up against what confronts you,
for what's been done's not what's done.
This land's so completely destroyed
that nothing remains, that not so much
as the black under a nail survives
what was fated. There's been such destruction
and violence there's no one left who's concerned,
no one who speaks, no one who weeps.
When clouds cover the sun, then everybody's
blind and deaf for lack of it
and nothing survives.
I show you a world in confusion,
with mankind living in graveyards.
We must begin the foundations
of our world all over again."

The Old Head Of Kinsale Says

I'm here in the Atlantic a long time:
two hundred and fifty million years.

My first and only tenants were migrant Celts
from the Mediterranean. They brought a light that
gave safe passage to passerby sailors forever.
They all left us in peace. Thus we have lived more than
two thousand years. No change in my bent grass hair.
It dies, regrows annually. No change in chough,
guillemot, gannet and fulmar, in kittiwake, razor-bill
and skylark that play about my head. No change
in bracken, bell heather and sea thrift in blossom
nor in beef or beastie from beef bullock to pygmy shrew.
No change in the migrating mammals that swim my myth
and no change in me, other than ages' natural weathering.

I have my natural heritage here. I shall keep it for mine.
A land that does not preserve its heritage is not a nation.

Printed in the United Kingdom
by Lightning Source UK Ltd.
122803UK00002B/292-303/A